ERNST ROWOHLT VERLAG · LEIPZIG

Zur Versendung liegt bereit:

FRANZ KAFKA

BETRACHTUNG

Einmalige Auflage von 800 in der Presse numerierten
Exemplaren. — Sorgfältiger Druck auf reinem Hadern-
papier durch die Offizin Poeschel & Trepte in Leipzig
In Japan-Broschur M 4.50 — In Halblederband M 6.50

Franz Kafka ist denen, die die Entwicklung unserer besten jungen
Dichter verfolgen, längst bekannt durch Novellen und Skizzen, die im
»Hyperion« und anderen Zeitschriften erschienen. Seine Eigenart, die
ihn dichterische Arbeiten immer und immer wieder durchzufeilen
zwingt, hielt ihn bisher von der Herausgabe von Büchern ab. Wir
freuen uns das Erscheinen des ersten Werkes dieses feinen, kultivierten
Geistes in unserem Verlage anzeigen zu können. Die Art der formal
feingeschliffenen, inhaltlich tief empfundenen und durchdachten Be-
trachtungen, die dieser Band vereinigt, stellt Kafka vielleicht neben
Robert Walser, von dem ihn doch wiederum in der dichterischen
Umgestaltung seelischer Erlebnisse tiefe Wesensunterschiede
trennen. Ein Autor und ein Buch, dem allseitig größtes
Interesse entgegengebracht wird.

Bis 1. Dezember bar bestellt: 40 %, Partie 7/6

Wir können der limitierten, einmaligen Auflage wegen à c. nur bei
gleichzeitiger Barbestellung und auch dann nur ganz beschränkt liefern.

D1722396

VITALIS

**BIBLIOTHECA
BOHEMICA**

MEDITATION

FRANZ KAFKA

MEDITATION

VITALIS

© Vitalis 2011 • Bibliotheca Bohemica • Cover design and illustrations by Karel Hruška • Translated from the German by Siegfried Mortkowitz • Afterword on the creation and impact of the text by Elisabeth Fuchs, translated by Alastair Matthews • Printed and bound in the European Union • ISBN 978-80-7253-255-1 • All rights reserved • www.vitalis-verlag.com

The publishers would like to thank Mr Hartmut Binder for permission to print the illustration on page 68 from his archive material. The remaining pictorial material is taken from the publisher's own archive of photographs and historical publications.

CONTENTS

CHILDREN ON THE COUNTRY ROAD

I heard the wagons drive past the garden fence, sometimes I also saw them through the gently moving gaps in the foliage. How the wood of their shafts and spokes creaked in the summer heat! Workers came from the field and laughed shamelessly.

I sat on our little swing, I was resting just then among the trees of my parents' garden.

In front of the fence, it just would not stop. Running children passed by in the wink of an eye; wagons carrying grain with men and women sitting on the sheaves and all around the flower-beds grew dark; towards evening I saw a gentleman with a cane walking along slowly and some girls, who came towards him arm in arm, greeted him and stepped aside into the grass.

Then birds flew up like spray, I followed them with my gaze, saw how they rose in one breath until I no longer believed that they were climbing, but that I was falling, and holding tight to the ropes I began to swing a little out of weakness. Soon I swung more vigorously while the air began to blow cooler and, in place of the flying birds, trembling stars appeared.

I was served my dinner by candlelight. Often I rested both arms on the tabletop and, already tired, bit into my buttered bread. The coarse-meshed curtains billowed in the warm wind, and sometimes someone passing outside held them with his hands if he wanted to see me better and to speak to me. Most of the time, the candle soon went out and the assembled gnats still hovered for a while in the candle's dark smoke. If someone questioned me from the window, I regarded him as if I were gazing at distant mountains or just staring into space, and he too didn't care whether he got an answer either.

If someone then jumped over the window ledge and announced that the others were already in front of the house, I, of course, stood up with a sigh.

"No, why are you sighing like that? What's happened? Is it some catastrophe that can never be undone? Will we never be able to recover from it? Is everything really lost?"

Nothing was lost. We ran to the front of the house. "Thank God, here you are at last!" – "You always come too late!" – "Me?" "Yes, you, stay at home if you don't want to come along." – "No mercy!" – "What? No mercy? What are you talking about?"

We rammed through the evening with our heads. There was no daytime and no nighttime. Soon, our waistcoat buttons were rubbing against each other like teeth, soon we were walking at a constant distance from each other, with fire in our mouths like animals in the tropics. Like cuirassiers in old wars, stamping and high up in the air, we urged each other

down the short street and, with this momentum in our legs, farther up the country road. A few stepped into the ditch at the side of the road, hardly had they vanished in front of the embankment than they were already standing like strangers up on the country path looking down.

"Hey, come down!" – "First you come up!" – "So that you can push us down, we wouldn't think of it, we're not idiots." – "You're cowards, you mean to say. Just come on up. Come on!" – "Really? You're going to push us down? That's what you think!"

We went on the attack, were struck in the chest and lay down, letting ourselves fall onto the grass in the ditch. Everything was equally warm, we felt no warmth, no cold in the grass, you only grew tired.

If you rolled onto your right side and put a hand under your ear, you would gladly have fallen asleep. But you wanted to pull yourself up again, with chin held high, only to fall instead into a deeper ditch. Then, with an arm held crosswise in front of you, your legs flapping crookedly, you wanted to leap into the air, only to fall with certainty into a still deeper ditch. And no one wanted to stop at all.

You hardly gave any thought about stretching out as much as possible, especially in the knees, to sleep properly in the last ditch, and instead lay on your back as if ill, wanting to weep. You blinked when, one time, a young boy, his elbow at his sides, jumped over us with his dark soles from the embankment to the street.

You already saw the moon quite high, a mail truck drove past in its light. A weak wind picked up all around, you even felt it in the ditch, and nearby the forest began to rustle. Then it was no longer so important to be alone.

"Where are you?" – "Come here!" – "All together!" – "Why are you hiding, stop that nonsense!" – "Don't you know that the mail has already passed by?" – "No, really? Already passed by?" – "Of course, it drove past while you were sleeping." – "I was sleeping? I don't believe it!" – "Be quiet, it's clear just from looking at you." – "Oh, really?" – "Come on!"

We ran closer together, some held hands, you couldn't hold your head high enough because we were going downhill. One let out an Indian war cry, our legs galloped as never before, when we jumped the wind picked us up by the hips. Nothing could have stopped us; we were running so fast that even when passing someone, we could fold our arms and calmly look around.

We stopped on the bridge over Wild Creek; those who had run farther, returned. The water below beat against the stones and roots, as if it were not already late evening. There was no reason why one of us did not jump onto the bridge railing.

From behind bushes in the distance, a train emerged, all the compartments were illuminated, the windows surely lowered. One of us

began to sing a popular song, but we all wanted to sing. We sang much faster than the train was going, we swung our arms because our voices were not enough, we came into a tumult of voices in which we were happy. If you blend your voice with others, you are caught as if on a fish hook.

So we sang, the forest behind us, into the ears of the distant travelers. The grown-ups were still awake in the village, the mothers were preparing the beds for the night.

It was already time. I kissed the one standing beside me, casually held out my hand to the next three, and began to run back the way we had come, no one called me. I turned at the first crossing, where they could no longer see me, and took the paths back into the forest. I made for the city in the south, about which people in our village say:

"Strange people live there! Just think, they don't sleep!"

"And why not?"

"Because they don't get tired."

"And why not?"

"Because they're fools."

"Don't fools get tired?"

"How can fools get tired?"

Unmasking of a Confidence Man

Finally, towards 10 o'clock in the evening, I arrived with a man I only knew fleetingly from ages ago – who this time had again joined me uninvited and dragged me through the streets for two hours – at the stately house to which I had been invited for a party.

"So," I said, and clapped my hands to signal that I absolutely had to leave him. I had already made a few, less resolute attempts. I was already very tired.

"Are you going up right away?" he asked. In his mouth I heard a sound like snapping teeth.

"Yes."

I was invited, I had told him that immediately. But I was invited to come up, and would gladly already have been there, and not to stand down here at the door and to look past the ears of the man facing me. And now even to fall silent together, as if we were determined to remain on this spot for a long time. And the houses all around quickly took their part in this silence, and the darkness above them as far as the stars. And the footsteps of invisible pedestrians whose direction one did not feel like guessing, the wind which buffeted the opposite side of the street again and again, a gramophone that was singing up against the closed window of some room – they announced themselves in this silence as if it had been their property always and for ever.

And my companion complied with it in his name and – after a smile – also in my name, stretched his right arm up the wall and leaned his face against it and closed his eyes.

But I did not see this smile to the end, because shame suddenly transformed me. From this smile I realized that he was a confidence man, nothing else. And I had already been in the city for months, had believed that I knew these confidence men through and through, how at night they come up to us out of side-streets like barkeepers, their hands oustretched, how they hang about poster pillars near which we stand, how they play hide-and-seek and spy with at least one eye from behind the pillar's curvature, how at intersections, when we grow anxious, they suddenly pop up in front of us on the pavement's edge! But I understood them so well, they were, after all, my first city acquaint-ances in the small pubs, and I was grateful to them for the first signs of a tenacity that I was so certain existed on earth that I had already begun to feel it in myself. How they confront-ed you, even if you had already escaped them long ago, that is, when there had been nothing to snare for a long time! How they refused to sit back or bend, but regarded you with looks that always, and if only from far away, per-suaded! And their method was always the same: They placed themselves before us as broadly as possible; tried to keep us from going where we wanted; prepared for us as a substitute a home in their own breast, and if in the end all our feelings rose up against them, they took it as an embrace into which they threw themselves, face first.

And this time I only recognized these old games after being with them for such a long time. I rubbed my fingertips against each other to erase the shame.

But my man was still leaning there as before, still took himself for a successful confidence man, and his self-satisfaction reddened his exposed cheek.

"I've got your number!" I said, and tapped him gently on the shoulder. Then I rushed up the stairs, and the unjustifiably loyal faces of the servants up in the anteroom delighted me like a lovely surprise. I regarded them all, one after the other, while someone removed my coat and dusted my boots. With a sigh of relief and stretched to my full height, I entered the hall.

THE UNEXPECTED STROLL

When in the evening it appears you have definitely decided to remain at home, have put on your dressing-gown, are sitting at the illuminated table after dinner and have begun some task or game after which you usually go to sleep, when the weather outside is unfriendly and makes staying at home self-evident, when you have now sat still at the table for so long that leaving would be certain to inspire general astonishment, when the staircase is already dark and the front entrance is locked, and when now, despite all of this, you stand up, suddenly anxious, change your clothes and immediately appear dressed for the street, explain that you must leave, and do it after a brief farewell, slamming shut the door to the flat with a haste corresponding to the annoyance you believe you have left behind, when you find yourself again in the street, with limbs that respond with exceptional mobility to the unexpected liberty you have secured for them, if through this one decision you feel gathered within you all decisiveness, if you realize with more than the usual significance that you possess more strength than you have need to bring about and bear the quickest change, and if you walk down the long streets in this mood – then for this evening you have completely withdrawn from your family, who veer towards the immaterial,

while you yourself, very firmly, black in out-
line, striking the back of your thighs, grow to
your true stature.

And everything is reinforced if, at this late
evening hour, you seek out a friend to see how
he is.

RESOLUTIONS

To lift yourself out of a miserable state must be easy, even with deliberate force. I tear myself from the armchair, walk around the table, make my head and neck move, bring fire to my eyes, tense the muscles around them. Work against every emotion, turbulently greet A. if he comes to see me now, amiably put up with B. in my room, absorb in long swallows everything that C. says despite the pain and effort it requires.

But even if I manage to bring it off, every unavoidable mistake begins to slow everything to a halt, the easy and the difficult, and I will have to circle back.

That's why the best advice remains to endure everything, to behave like a ponderous mass and, if you feel you are being blown away, not let yourself be lured into a single unnecessary step, to regard your oposite with the gaze of an animal, to feel no regret, in brief, to suppress with your own hand whatever ghostly remains of life, which means increasing the terminal peace of the grave and letting nothing exist but that.

One characteristic gesture of this condition is to run your little finger over your eyebrows.

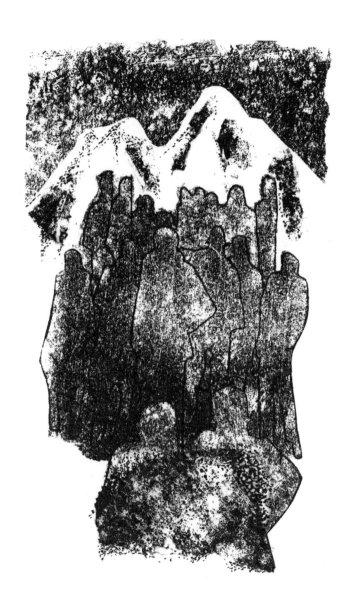

Excursion to the Mountains

I don't know," I shouted soundlessly. "I just don't know. If nobody comes, well, then nobody comes. I haven't harmed anyone, nobody has harmed me, but nobody wants to help me. Lots of nobody. But that's not how it is. Only that nobody is helping me – otherwise lots of nobody would be nice. I'd be very happy – and why not? – to go on an excursion with a bunch of these nobodies. To the mountains, of course, where else? How these nobodies would jostle each other, these many crosswise stretched and arms coupled together, these many feet separated by tiny steps! Of course, they're all in evening dress. We're all going along so-so-so, the wind blows through the gaps between our appendages. In the mountains our throats free up. It is a miracle that we don't sing."

A Bachelor's Misfortune

It seems so dreadful to remain a bachelor, an old man toiling to maintain his dignity while asking to be invited whenever you want to spend an evening with people, to be ill and, for an entire week, stare at the empty room from the corner where the bed stands, always to say good-bye at the street door, never to push yourself up the stairs beside your wife, to have only side doors in your room that lead to the flats of strangers, to carry your dinner home in one hand, having to gawk at the children of strangers and not always being allowed to repeat: "I have none," to model your appearance and behaviour after the memory of one or two bachelors from your youth.

That's how it will be, except that in reality you will stand there yourself, with a body and a real head, that means also a forehead, which you can smack with your hand.

THE MERCHANT

It's possible that some people feel sorry for me, but I felt nothing of it. My small business fills me with troubles that hurt me internally, at the forehead and temples, but without providing me with the prospect of satisfaction, because my business is small.

Five hours ahead of time I must make decisions, jog the caretaker's memory, warn him of the mistakes I am afraid he will make and calculate in one season the fashions of the next, not what will be popular with the people in my circles but with inaccessible peasants in the countryside.

Strangers have my money; I cannot figure out their affairs; I have no idea of the misfortune that could befall them; how could I prevent it! Perhaps they've become extravagant and are throwing a banquet in a garden restaurant and others are at the banquet to pause for a while on their flight to America.

When, on a workday evening, the business is locked up and I suddenly see hours before me during which I will not be able to work for the incessant requirements of my shop, then the excitement that I projected far ahead of me in the morning tosses itself back like a returning high tide, but cannot last in me and carries me haphazardly along.

And, nevertheless, I cannot use this mood at all and can only go home, because my face and hands are dirty and sweaty, my clothes are stained and dusty, I have my working cap on my head and wear boots that have been scratched by packing-crate nails. Then I walk as if on waves, snapping the fingers of both hands, and stroke the hair of children I pass along the way.

But the way is too short. I reach home immediately, open the door to the lift and enter.

I see that I am suddenly alone now. Others who have to climb the stairs, growing a bit tired in the process, must wait with quickening breath until the door is opened for them, have therefore a reason to be angry and impatient, now enter the anteroom, where they hang their hats, and they are not alone until they walk through the hallway, pass several glass doors and come into their own room.

But in the lift I'm alone at once and, down on my knees, look in the small mirror. As the lift begins to rise, I say,

"Be quiet, go back, do you want to reach the shadow of the trees, behind the room curtains, or the vaulted arbour?"

I talk with my teeth and the banisters glide past the panes of frosted glass like falling water.

"Fly away; may your wings, which I have never seen, carry you to the village vale or to Paris, if that's where you want to go.

But enjoy the view from the window when the processions come from all three streets, converge upon each other, pass through one another and let the empty square appear again among their last rows. Wave your handker-chiefs, be horrified, be moved, praise the beau-tiful lady who drives past.

Cross the brook by the wooden bridge, nod at the bathing children and marvel at the Hurrah! of the thousand sailors on the distant battleship.

Follow only the inconspicuous man, and when you have shoved him into a doorway, rob him and watch him, everybody with their hands in their pockets, as he goes sadly on his way down the street on the left.

The police, scattered on their galloping horses, rein in their animals and force you back. Let them, the empty streets will make them unhappy, I know it. See, they are already riding away in pairs, slowly around corners, swiftly across the squares."

Then I must get out, send the lift down again, ring the doorbell, and the maid opens the door as I say good evening.

Looking Out Absentmindedly

What will we do on these spring days that are so quickly approaching? Earlier today the sky was grey, but if you now go to the window, you are surprised and rest your cheek against its handle.

Below, you see the light of the, indeed, already setting sun on the face of the little girl, who strolls and looks around aimlessly, and at the same time you see upon everything the shadow of a man who follows her at a quicker pace.

Then the man has passed and the child's face is very bright.

THE WAY HOME

Regard the persuasiveness of the air after a thunderstorm! My merits become evident and overwhelm me, though admittedly I put up little resistance.

I march, and my tempo is the tempo of this side of the street, of this whole street, of this quarter. I am, justifiably, responsible for all the knocks on doors, upon tabletops, for all toasts, for the lovers in their beds, in the scaffolding of new constructions, pressed against houses in dark streets, on the ottomans in bordellos.

I weigh my past against my future, find both splendid, cannot choose one over the other, and am forced to criticise only the injustice of Providence which so clearly favours me.

Only when I enter my room am I a bit pensive, but without having found anything worth thinking about while climbing the stairs. It does not help me much when I open wide the window and hear music still playing in a garden.

THE PASSERS-BY

When at night you go walking in the street and a man, already visible from afar – for the street goes uphill and the moon is full – runs toward us, we will not seize him, even if he is weak and shabby, even if someone else is running behind him and yells, we will rather let him run on.

Because it is night and we can't help it that the street under a full moon goes uphill, and furthermore, perhaps these two have arranged this chase for their own amusement, perhaps the two are pursuing a third, perhaps the first man, although innocent, is being pursued, perhaps the second wants to kill him and we will become accomplices to the murder, perhaps the two are not aware of each other and each of them is only running home to bed at his own risk, perhaps they are sleepwalkers, perhaps the first man is armed.

And, finally, shouldn't we be tired, haven't we drunk a lot of wine? We're glad that we can't even see the second man any more.

THE PASSENGER

I am standing on the platform of a tram and am totally uncertain in regard to my status in this world, in this city, in my family. I couldn't even incidentally specify what demands I could justifiably make in any direction. I cannot at all account for the fact that I am standing on this platform, holding on to this strap, letting myself be carried by this tram, that people make way for the tram or walk along quietly or pause before shop windows. It's true that no one demands it of me, but that doesn't matter.

The tram nears a stop, a young woman positions herself near the steps, ready to get off. She appears to me so distinctly, as if I had felt her all over. She is dressed in black, the pleats of her skirt scarcely stir, her blouse is tight and has a collar of white fine-meshed lace, she presses her left hand flat against the wall, the umbrella in her right hand rests on the second step from the top. Her face is brown, her nose, slightly pinched at the sides, is round and broad at the tip. She has a lot of brown hair and scattered little hairs on her right temple. Her small ear is set close against her head, but as I am standing near her, I can see the whole back of the outer ear and the shadow at its root.

At the time I asked myself: How is it that she is not astonished at herself, that she keeps her mouth shut and says nothing about it?

CLOTHES

Often, when I see clothes with many pleats, ruffles and tassels that fit nicely over beautiful bodies, then I think that they will not remain like that for long, but will become so creased that they can't be smoothed out, attract dust that will lie so thick in the decorations that it cannot be removed, and that no one would want to be so dispirited and ridiculous as to wear each day the same expensive dress from morning to evening.

But I see beautiful girls with many enticing muscles and delicate ankles and tight skin and masses of fine hair, who nevertheless appear day in and day out in the same natural fancy dress, always press the same face against the same hands and let it be reflected in their mirrors.

But sometimes, when they return late at night from some party, it appears in the mirror worn-out, puffy, dusty, already seen by everyone and hardly fit to be worn any more.

The Rejection

When I meet a beautiful young woman and ask her, "Be so good and come with me," and she passes me by without a word, she means by that:

"You are no duke with a lofty name, no strapping American with an Indian's build, with level, placid eyes, with skin massaged by the air of the prairies and the rivers that flow through them, you have made no journeys to the great lakes, or upon them, wherever they may be. So, I ask you, why should I, a beautiful young woman, go with you?"

"You forget that no grand automobile conveys you, swaying in its long lunges, through the street; I don't see an escort of neatly dressed men murmuring blessings and following you in a precise semi-circle; your breasts are nicely arranged in your bodice, but your thighs and hips make up for this modesty; you are wearing a taffeta dress with pleats like those which delighted us all last autumn, and still you smile – wrapped in this mortal danger – now and then.

"Yes, we're both right, and to avoid becoming irrefutably aware of it, shouldn't we rather go home alone?"

Some Thoughts
for Amateur Jockeys

If you think about it, nothing can tempt one to want to come in first in a horserace.

The fame of being known as the best jockey in the country is too much of a joy when the orchestra strikes up to be able to prevent repentance on the morning after.

The envy of your rivals, cunning, fairly influential men, must torment us in the narrow cordon through which we now ride after leaving the course which soon grew empty in front of us except for a few outdistanced riders, who shrank as they approached the horizon.

Many of our friends rush to collect their winnings and shout their Hurrah! at us over their shoulders from distant betting windows; but our best friends didn't wager anything on our horse at all, fearful of having to be angry with us if they lost, but now that our horse has come in first and they have won nothing, they turn their backs when we pass and prefer to gaze out at the stands.

The trailing rivals, firmly in their saddles, try to grasp their bad luck and the injustice that was somehow dealt them; they are putting a new face on things, as if another race were about to start, a serious one after this child's play.

To many ladies, the winner seems ridiculous because he puffs himself up but still does not know how to deal with the incessant hand-shakes, saluting, bowing and waving-into-the-distance, while the vanquished have shut their mouths and gently pat the necks of their mostly whinnying horses.

Finally, rain even begins to fall from the now overcast sky.

WINDOW ONTO THE STREET

Whoever leads a solitary life, yet wants now and then to attach himself somewhere, whoever – depending on the changes in the time of day, the weather, the state of one's business and the like – wants to see, without having to ask, any arm at all which he could grasp, he will not be able to carry on very long without a window onto the street. And if he doesn't feel like looking at anything and only goes to the window-sill a tired man, his eyes flitting from the public to the sky, and he does not want to look out and has bent his head back slightly, he will still be carried away by the horses with their train of wagons and noise, and therefore, at last, towards human harmony.

The Wish to Become an Indian

If only you were an Indian, instantly alert, and on a galloping horse, leaning into the rushing air, again and again trembling over the trembling ground, until you leave the spurs behind, for there were no spurs, until you throw away the reins, for there were no reins, and you scarcely saw the land lying before you like a smooth-mown heath, already without a horse's neck and a horse's head.

THE TREES

For we are like tree trunks in the snow. They appear to lie flat and with a small push one should be able to dislodge them. No, it can't be done, because they are firmly joined to the ground. But, look, even that only appears to be so.

BEING UNHAPPY

When it already had become unbearable – once toward evening in November – and I paced over the narrow carpet in my room as if on a racetrack, startled by the sight of the illuminated street, turned again and found a new goal in the back of my room, in the depths of my mirror, and screamed just to hear the scream, to which nothing replies and which nothing can rob of its force, so that it ascends without counterweight, and cannot cease even if it falls mute, then a door opened in the wall so hastily, because haste was required, and even the draught-horses down on the cobblestones reared up like horses driven wild in battle, their throats exposed.

Like a small ghost, a child emerged out of the pitch-dark corridor, in which the lamp was still not lit, and stopped on tiptoe on an indiscernibly quivering floorboard. Immediately dazzled by the twilight of my room, she quickly made as if to cover her face with her hands, but abruptly calmed herself with a glance at the window, where behind its crossed sash the rising vapour of the streetlamps had finally settled beneath the darkness. With her right elbow pressed against the wall, she held herself upright at the open door and let the draught from outside pass over her ankles, and her throat too, and also along her temples.

I briefly looked at her, then said "Hello" and took my jacket from the oven hood because I did not want to stand there half-naked. I kept my mouth open for a while, so that my agitation could dissipate through it. There was a bad taste to my siliva, my eyelashes quivered, in brief this unexpected visit was just what I needed.

The child was still standing in the same spot against the wall, she had her right hand pressed against the plaster and could not get enough, her cheeks all red, of rubbing her fingertips over the rough white-washed wall. I said: "Do you really want to see me? Is it no mistake? There's nothing easier than to make a mistake in this big house. My name is So-and-so, I live in the third floor. So am I the one you want to visit?"

"Be quiet, be quiet," the child said over her shoulder. "It's alright."

"Then come farther into my room. I'd like to shut the door."

"I've just shut the door. Don't bother. Just relax anyway."

"It's no bother. But a lot of people live along this corridor, all of them are acquaintances of mine, of course; most of them are now coming home from work; if they hear people talking in a room, they think they have the right to just open the door and see what's going on. That's just how it is. These people have left their daily work behind; who would they kowtow to during their temporary evening liberty!

And, by the way, you know it too. Let me shut the doors."

"What's wrong with you? What's your problem? I don't care if the whole house comes in here. And to repeat: I've already shut the door. Do you think you're the only one who can shut the door? I've even locked them with the key."

"Then it's okay. That's all I want. You didn't really have to lock it. And now that you're here, just make yourself comfortable. You're my guest. You can trust me completely. Make yourself at home and don't be afraid. I won't force you to stay or to go away. Do I really have to say that? Do you know me so little?"

"No. You really didn't have to say that. Furthermore, you shouldn't have said it! I'm a child; why be so ceremonious with me?"

"It's not that bad. Of course, a child. But you're not that small. You're already all grown up. If you were a young woman, you wouldn't be allowed simply to lock yourself in a room with me."

"We don't have to worry about that. I only wanted to say: It's little protection for me that I know you so well, it only relieves you of the effort of lying to me. In spite of that, you give me compliments. Stop it; I urge you to stop it. And there's also the fact that I don't know you everywhere and always, especially in this darkness. It would be much better if you had the lights turned on. No, better not.

At any rate, I'll remember that you've already threatened me."

"What? I threatened you? But, listen, I'm so happy that you've come at last. I say 'at last' because it's already so late. I don't understand why you've come so late. It is possible that, in my delight, I talked indiscriminately and that you've misunderstood. I'll admit ten times that I spoke like that, yes, I threatened you with whatever you want – only let's not quarrel, for Heaven's! But how could you think that? How could you hurt me like that? Why do you want to spoil this brief moment of your presence here with all your might? A stranger would be more accommodating than you."

"I believe that; that was not a particularly brilliant statement. Just by nature I am as close to you as a stranger could ever be. And you know that, why the heavy heart? Tell me that you want to play a comedy and I'll leave at once."

"Aha. Even that you dare to say to me? You're a little too bold. After all, you're in my room. You're rubbing your fingers over my wall like mad. My room, my wall! And, what's more, what you're saying is ridiculous, not just fresh. You say that your nature is forcing you to talk to me like that? Your nature? Really? Your nature is forcing you? How nice of your nature. Your nature is mine, and I am by nature friendly to you, you shouldn't be any different."

"Is that friendly?"

"I'm talking about earlier."

"Do you know what I'll be like later?"

"I don't know a thing."

And I went to the bedside table and lit the candle there. At that time, I had neither gas nor electric light in my room. I sat for a while at the table until I grew tired of that too, put on my overcoat, took the hat from the sofa and blew out the candle. As I was leaving, I tripped on the leg of an armchair.

On the stairs I met a tenant from the same floor.

"You're going out again, you rascal?" he asked while resting with his legs stretched over two steps.

"What can I do?" I said. "I just had a ghost in my room."

"You say that with the same dissatisfaction as if you'd found a hair in your soup."

"You're joking. But remember, a ghost is a ghost."

"Very true. But what if one didn't believe in ghosts at all?"

"Do you really think I believe in ghosts? But what good does this not believing do me?"

"Very simple. You just don't have to be afraid when a ghost actually comes to visit you."

"Yes, but this is only the incidental fear. The real fear is the fear of what caused the apparition. And this fear remains. I have it in me in a big way." Out of nervousness, I began to search through all my pockets.

"Since you were not afraid of the apparition, you could easily have asked it about its cause!"

"You've obviously never talked to ghosts. You can never get a straight answer from them. It's an endless discussion. These ghosts seem to doubt their existence more than we do, and no wonder, considering how frail they are."

"But I've heard that you can fatten them up."

"You're well informed there. You can. But who'll do it?"

"Why not? If it's a female ghost, for example," he said and swung himself onto the top step.

"Oh," I said, "but even then it's not worth the trouble."

I remembered something. My acquaintance was already so high up that he had to duck under an arch in the stairwell in order to see me. "But despite that," I shouted, "if you take away my ghost up there, then it's all over between us forever."

"But it was just a joke," he said and drew back his head.

"Then it's okay," I said and without further bother could actually have gone for a walk then. But because I felt so forsaken, I preferred to go back up, and went to bed.

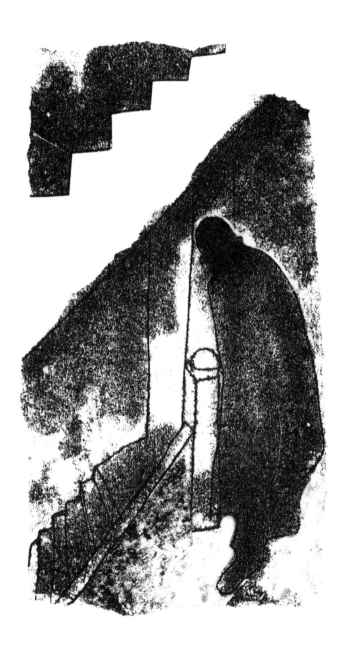

ALBERT EHRENSTEIN
ON KAFKA'S *MEDITATION*

A strangely great, strangely refined book by an ingeniously sensitive writer. Franz Kafka is – in contrast to other Praguers – a discreet man. "Whoever recognises him, greets him." One never knows from his sketches wheter "she" is named Emma and "he" Erwin. No "he" and "she" is pretended, they are not professionally and "suspensefully" prepared in the flesh and precisely realized. Kafka is discreet, he uses the alphabet only allusively, he restrains himself deliberately and from a tidyness of feeling. He has always been far removed from writing a book – basically always only a plain book – single-mindedly, administrating it and piling it up by force of organisation. A sign of this, as of every lost masterpiece, is still that it is indescribable and inaccessible to the analysis of your run-of-the-mill commentator, it exists for itself and for some time rests unimpeachably on, and persists in, its own merits – and is nevertheless so fragile that the next breeze could carry it away.

Kafka delivers small acts, small emotions, sensitively and timidly, like the rare images of a rational, indestructible dream. His nobly restrained book fades in gently wonderful arabesques, in the asides made by a lodger an subtenant of life who is ready to disappear and hard to find. Such depressing (but illuminating) books are written only in political, but not expansionary, and not very aggressive countries. Kafka only asserts himself, so to speak, vis-á-vis his notebook. What he says sounds as if it had been whispered by one of the few dear, quiet existences that have been pushed to the wall and which are only still found in the kingdoms and nations represented by the Austrian Imperial Parliament. A rare lyrical prose, without punch lines, less cleverly witty than that of Peter Altenberg.

A remarkably great, remarkably refined book by an ingeniously sensitive writer!

Albert Ehrenstein,
in *Berliner Tagblatt*

16 April 1913

OTHER BOOKS BY AND ABOUT FRANZ KAFKA FROM VITALIS

"My book, my little book, my pages
have been gladly accepted"

Franz Kafka to Felice Bauer

№ 269, 18. November 1912.   künftig erscheinende Bücher.   Rheinstra[ß]e I. k. Preuß. Buchhandl. 14607

ERNST ROWOHLT VERLAG · LEIPZIG

Zur Versendung liegt bereit:

FRANZ KAFKA
BETRACHTUNG

Einmalige Auflage von 800 in der Presse numerierten
Exemplaren. — Sorgfältiger Druck auf reinem Hader-
papier durch die Offizin Poeschel & Trepte in Leipzig
In Japan-Broschur M 4.50 — In Halblederband M 6.50

Franz Kafka ist denen, die die Entwicklung unserer besten jungen
Dichter verfolgen, längst bekannt durch Novellen und Skizzen, die im
»Hyperion« und anderen Zeitschriften erschienen. Seine Eigenart, die
ihn dichterische Arbeiten immer und immer wieder durchzufeilen
zwingt, hielt ihn bisher von der Herausgabe von Büchern ab. Wir
freuen uns das Erscheinen des ersten Werkes dieses feinen, kultivierten
Geistes in unserem Verlage anzeigen zu können. Die Art der formal
feingeschliffenen, inhaltlich tief empfundenen und durchdachten Be-
trachtungen, die dieser Band vereinigt, stellt Kafka vielleicht neben
Robert Walser, von dem ihn doch wiederum in der dichterischen
Umgestaltung seelischer Erlebnisse tiefe Wesensunterschiede
trennen. Ein Autor und ein Buch, dem allseitig größtes
Interesse entgegengebracht wird.

Bis 1. Dezember bar bestellt: 40 %, Partie 7/6

Wir können der limitierten, einmaligen Auflage wegen à c. nur bei
gleichzeitiger Barbestellung und auch dann nur ganz beschränkt liefern.

An announcement placed in the *Börsenblatt* by
the Ernst Rowohlt Verlag on 18 November 1912.

The air in the engine room of the Prager Asbestwerke Hermann & Co. is almost unbearable. The heat of the August day forces its way in from the factory floor, and there is a smell of gas. The foremen and the stokers have been working feverishly for two hours now. They curse: the engine just won't start! Franz Kafka is standing next to them. He is unable to help, for he knows nothing about how the machines work. But he is nonetheless the "& Co." on the sign outside the asbestos factory: Dr Franz Kafka, twenty-nine years old, insurance officer, and, for the last six months, non-active partner in this factory belonging to his brother-in-law, Karl Hermann. With its fourteen engines it is at the cutting edge of technology in 1912, and he is the superior of the twenty-five workers employed in the factory. But there are far more important things for him to think about. Kafka's mind is with his manuscripts, lying on his desk at home, which he has to go over and put in order. A young publisher called Ernst Rowohlt has taken an interest in the texts and wants to print them in book form – Franz Kafka's very first book of his own.

Kafka had started writing much earlier, when he was still a grammar-school student at the Altstädter Deutsches Gymnasium (German Secondary School) in his

Left: The building in the Prague suburb of Žižkov that was once home to the Prager Asbestwerke Hermann & Co.

Above right: Advertisement for the Prager Asbestwerke.

Below right: Franz Kafka as a grammar-school student.

home town of Prague. These first works consisted mainly of attempts to confront difficulties he was facing, to come to terms with himself as he grew up. None have survived; after all, this young writer had always been so critical of his own work that he would not hesitate to destroy it if he was not convinced it was a complete success. His first more substantial works began to appear when he was studying law – the first version of *Description of a Struggle,* for example, and then, after he had graduated with a doctorate in law in 1906, the fragmentary *Wedding Preparations in the Country.* A short time later, some of his short prose pieces were published for the first time as "Meditation" in the magazine *Hyperion.* From 1908, however, Franz Kafka worked at the Arbeiter-Unfall-Versicherungs-Anstalt für das Königreich Böhmen (Workers' Accident Insurance Company for the Kingdom of Bohemia) in Prague, an insurance institute where his time was spent writing letters and reports; it was often the night hours alone that remained for literary work now, since his family expected him to turn his attention to the asbestos factory as often as possible when his afternoons were free.

Prager Asbestwerke Hermann & Co., Prag

offerieren Wiederverkäufern bei promptester Bedienung in erstklassigen Fabrikaten

Asbest- und Asbest-Kautschukwaren jeder Art. ∞ Technische Fettpräparate. Stopfbüchsenpackungen. ∞ Hochdruck- platten. ∞ Isoliermaterialien.

Even a short time after the plant was founded, Kafka had remarked in his diary that "the factory torments me. Why did I stay quiet when they committed me to working there in the afternoon. No one uses force to make me go, true, but father uses reproaches, Karl silence and my own feelings of guilt. I know nothing about the factory and was standing around useless and impotent during the committee's visit this morning."[1]

How good Kafka must have felt, then, when he was able to abandon the asbestos factory, the insurance office, and the reproachful glances of his family for a change and leave Prague with Max Brod, his friend and even then a well-known writer. The opportunity to do so had presented itself only a short time ago, early in the summer of 1912, when a doctor advised Kafka to take a recuperative cure "of at least four weeks at a well-run establishment […] due to digestive problems, low body-weight, and a series of nervous complaints".[2] At first, Kafka wanted to use this special break to make a short trip to Weimar on holiday with Max Brod, where he hoped to visit such places as Goethe's house, Schiller's house, and the famous Großherzogliche Bibliothek. Brod, however, had more in mind: when the friends stopped in Leipzig on their way to Weimar, he arranged a meeting with the publisher Ernst Rowohlt. Max Brod was aware of Kafka's extremely critical attitude toward his own literary output; now, he must have thought to himself, was the time to give his friend a helping hand on the way to success. Rowohlt's partner, Kafka's later publisher

Left: The writer Max Brod, who was a friend of Kafka and later edited his works.

Right: A drawing of Goethe's garden house by Kafka.

Kurt Wolff, describes in his *Autoren, Bücher, Abenteuer (Authors, Books, Adventures)* what happened in the publisher's office in Leipzig that afternoon on 29 June 1912: "In the afternoon, Max Brod, who already had connections with the publisher, brought Kafka into the shabby little office […]. I would be the last to seek to belittle what Max Brod did for his friend in life and in death – it cannot be valued highly enough – so I hope he will forgive me when I say that, as soon as they appeared, I had the indelible impression that an impresario was presenting me with the star he had discovered. Of course, that was precisely the case, and if the impression was an embarrassing one, then it was embarrassing because of Kafka's nature […]. Alas, how he suffered. Silent, awkward, tender, vulnerable, timid like a grammar-school student facing his examiners, convinced he would never be able to meet the expectations raised by the praise of the impresario […]. As he was leaving on that day in June 1912, Kafka made a remark that I have never before or since heard from any other author, a remark that has therefore been inextricably linked with the one and only Kafka in my mind: 'I will be far more grateful to you for returning my manuscripts than for publishing them.'"[3] In his travel diary,

The entrance to the Jungborn nature therapy sanatorium in Stapelburg.

Kafka too described that first meeting, observing drily and with a certain amount of disbelief: "R. is fairly serious about wanting a book from me."[4]

In the immediate future, though, there was no time to reflect on the full significance of this meeting with the two publishers. There was far too much culture to discover in the city of Weimar; the acquaintance of Margarethe Kirchner, daughter of the custodian of Goethe's house, too, took up Kafka's time so that the meeting with the Leipzig publishers fell into the background for the present. Kafka also had a stay of almost three weeks in the Jungborn nature therapy sanatorium in the Harz Mountains ahead of him. He used these weeks of rest to continue with the now lost first version of *The Man Who Disappeared,* on which he had been working since the previous winter. When his attempts to write failed to progress smoothly, Kafka was again plagued by doubts about his ability as a writer, which cast the planned edition of *Meditation* into uncertainty. Nonetheless, at the beginning of August, after returning to Prague, he began selecting pieces of work that would be suitable for publication.

It is evening. The hours of torment in the factory are over, and Kafka is in his room in his parents' apartment in the street called the Niklasstraße. The droning engines and the stinging smell of gas are far away, and the only sounds are the soft rustle of the pages and the scratch of pen on paper. Kafka is busy extracting passages from his early novella *Description of a Struggle* and reworking them into self-contained texts. It is already eight years since he began work on the novella. Then, in 1904, Russia and Japan had just engaged in war; the world has not become more peaceful in the meantime. The situation in the Balkans, for example, is becoming ominously tense, so you can sense, even in 1912, that the way that will lead to the First World War two years later has already been laid – at least if, like Kafka, you pay careful attention to developments in world affairs.

Kafka's own life, too, has changed in the previous eight years. After obtaining his

Left and below:
The early twentieth century was characterized by considerable contrasts. Opulence, fashion, and recreation were prominent in privileged sections of society, while political conflicts were becoming more and more intense all over the world.

doctorate in 1906, Kafka had first completed his obligatory year of legal work experience, initially at the district court on the Obstmarkt and then, after half a year, at the criminal court on the Karlsplatz, before finally beginning work as a temporary employee at the private insurance company Assicurazioni Generali on Wenceslas Square. A twelve-hour day was not unusual then, and there was little hope of regular writing with only seven days' holiday each year. Since summer 1908, though, Kafka had been employed at the Arbeiter-Unfall-Versicherungsanstalt and was able to leave work at 2 p.m. every day. The asbestos factory summoned him now and then after 1911, but Kafka nonetheless had more time now to take a walk with his friend Max Brod, to spend the evening discussing literature in a coffee-house, perhaps with Franz Werfel and his circle – and to write at night. Consequently, Kafka was able to return not only to old manuscripts when searching for texts to include in his *Meditation,* but also to much more recent work such as "The Sudden Walk", which he had set down in his diary early in 1912.

Three days after that afternoon in the engine room of the asbestos factory, on 13 August 1912, Kafka set off to see Max Brod and discuss the manuscript he had prepared for book publication with him. When he entered Brod's home, the cousin of Brod's brother-in-law was sitting at the table: Felice Bauer. "Bony empty face," Kafka later observed in his diary. "Nose almost broken, blond hair stiff and rather plain, chin strong. I looked at her more carefully for the first time as I was sitting down; by the time I was seated my judgement could not be shaken."[5] There is nothing in these remarks to suggest the role Felice was to play in the subsequent years of Kafka's life. He would write over five hundred letters to her; twice, in 1914 and 1917, he would become engaged with her, twice he would call off the engagement. On that August Tuesday, though, she looked pale and insignificant to him, like a "servant-girl".[6] And yet, Felice must have made some

Left: The ornate offices of Assicurazioni Generali on Wenceslas Square in Prague.

Right: Felice and Franz in their engagement photo of 1917.

kind of immediate impression on Kafka, for the next day he was not sure whether he had really been concentrating properly when discussing his texts with Max Brod. He wrote to Brod: "Good morning! Dear Max, I was under the influence of the girl when we were arranging the pieces yesterday; it's quite possible that this has led to some kind of mistake, a foolishness in the arrangement that isn't apparent at first glance. Please, look into this, and allow me to thank you for it as part of that really big thank you I owe you."[7]

Max Brod, however, was still well satisfied with the arrangement of the pieces and sent them to the publishers in Leipzig that very day. At the same time, Kafka wrote a letter to Ernst Rowohlt, saying: "I am now sending you the small prose collection that you desired to see. It should be enough to make up a small book, I think. While putting it together for this purpose, I was sometimes faced with the choice between doing right by my own sense of responsibility and the desire that I too might have a book in your fine collection. Certainly, my decisions were not always the purest. However, I would now be happy if the things pleased you just so much for you to publish them. In the end, even the greatest experience and understanding are not enough to reveal what is bad in these things at first glance. After all, the most widespread individuality among writers lies in the fact that they all conceal their bad sides in their own special ways."[8]

Rowohlt and Wolff liked the "things". They conclusively agreed to print them. Despite his reservations, this acceptance released enormous energy in Kafka. His first decision was to send a letter to Felice Bauer in Berlin, where the young woman was working as a secretary. This was the first step on the path that turned a passing acquaintance into a fiancée. Just two days after this first letter, in the night of 22 to 23 September 1912, he experienced a creative outburst that he had never known before: he set the story *The Judgement* down on paper in no more than eight hours. As for his *Meditation,* all that was left was to find, together with his publishers in Leipzig, "a suitable typeface and felicitous format that will allow us to give the rather small manuscript a more substantial form".[9] They managed to solve this problem as well, so that, in mid-October, Kafka received a sample about which he later wrote to Felice Bauer: "Its elegance is a touch overdone, no doubt, and it would be more appropriate to the tablets of Moses than to my little diversions. But it's going to be printed like this now."[10]

Franz Kafka in 1910.

Kafka finally held the first copy of *Meditation* in his hands in December 1912. It was dedicated to his friend Max Brod, whose work as an intermediary had made the publication possible in the first place and who had given Kafka such help on that August evening when Felice Bauer had been visiting the Brods. It was to her, at once, that Kafka sent the first copy: "Please, be good to my poor book! After all, these are the few pages that you saw me arranging on our evening. Then you were judged 'not fit' to see them, foolish and vengeful beloved! Now they belong to you as to no one else, unless I snatch them jealously from your hand to be held by you alone rather than having to share my place with an old, tiny book. I wonder whether you will be able to see how the individual pieces differ in age. There is one of them, for example, that is certainly 8 to 10 years old. Show the whole thing to as few people as possible, so that they don't spoil your desire for me. Good night, dearest, good night."[11]

The first review was not long in coming. On 20 December, Franz Kafka's first published work was mentioned in a discussion of several books in the Jewish

FRANZ KAFKA

BETRACHTUNG

MDCCCXIII

ERNST ROWOHLT VERLAG

LEIPZIG

Left: The first copy of Kafka's *Meditation*, bearing a dedication to Felice: "For Miss Felice Bauer, to endear myself to her with these memories of old unhappy times."

Right: The logo of the *Prager Tagblatt*, where Kafka's *Meditation* was reviewed.

Prager Tagblatt

Morgen-Ausgabe.

weekly *Selbstwehr (Self-defence)*. Readers were told that "Kafka's small meditations are something previously unknown in German literature; I cannot think of any precedent. Touching so gently on some passages of Brod, with a force that is often truly remarkable they go beyond him to become something special in the art with which they break a momentary feeling or mood down into its most basic elements and, in most cases, bind them to things, and with the devotion with which they set themselves inside people and things."[12] In January 1913, the *Prager Tagblatt (Prague Daily)* printed a piece by Kurt Tucholsky, then twenty-three years old, which said: "There is melody in what he says, and even if it is possible to dispute the legitimacy of such a man of letters, to do so is not to make a judgement about Kafka's great ability."[13] Kafka felt that the review by Otto Pick, a Prague writer among his circle of friends, was "excessive in its praise";[14] it did, after all, speak of "unbelievable maturity, the ease of masterly French prose, rhythmical, like the laments of lonely girls".[15] This treatment, however, was outdone by the outpouring of enthusiasm with which Max Brod greeted the publication of his friend's first book: "I could well conceive of someone coming across this book […] and from that moment on changing his whole life, becoming a new person. Such is the openness and sweet strength of these few short prose pieces. At first, it is not possible to grasp them, to analyse them. I know of no modern or ancient author with whom Kafka has anything significant in common. […] It is the love of the divine, of the absolute, that speaks out of every line."[16] A letter to Felice Bauer tells us how Kafka responded to this review: "I could have done with a hole to hide at noon today: I read Max's discussion of my book in the new copy of *März [March]*. I knew that the piece was going to be published, but I hadn't seen it. A few discussions of the book have already been printed, only by people I know, of course, useless in their exaggerated praise, useless in their comments, and explicable only as signs of misguided affection, of an excessive importance attached to the printed word, of a misunderstanding of the relationship between literature and the reading public. […] But Max's discussion goes through the roof. The friendship he feels with me has its root on the most human level, long before literature begins, and is thus already mighty before literature even starts to breathe, and so he overrates me in a way that makes me ashamed and vain and arrogant, while he, of course, with his knowledge of art and his own strength, has practically surrounded himself with the true opinion, which is nothing but an opinion. But he still writes like that."[17]

Reading these reviews may give the impression that Kafka was a celebrated writer from that point on, but in reality he remained entirely unknown to the general public for many years, far beyond his death in 1924. Kafka once remarked to his friend Rudolf Fuchs with respect to *Meditation* that "there were eleven books at André's. I bought ten myself. I would just like to know who has the eleventh."[18] It was twelve years until the first edition of eight hundred copies was sold out. And so Kafka was left with no choice but to continue his work at the insurance institute and relegate writing to the hours of evening and the night. His frustration with the asbestos factory, though, did not continue for too long: Karl Hermann's brother Paul soon took over some of Kafka's duties, and when the First World War broke out, the unfavourable conditions actually caused the factory to close. Afternoons in the engine room became a thing of the past.

NOTES

[1] Diary, 28 December 1911.
[2] Klaus Hermsdorf, "Briefe des Versicherungsangestellten Franz Kafka", *Sinn und Form* 9 (1957), 665–66.
[3] Kurt Wolff, *Autoren, Bücher, Abenteuer: Betrachtungen und Erinnerungen eines Verlegers* (Berlin, 1965), p. 68.
[4] Weimar-Jungborn travel diary, 29 June 1912.
[5] Diary, 20 August 1912.
[6] Diary, 20 August 1912.
[7] Letter to Max Brod, 14 August 1912.
[8] Letter to Ernst Rowohlt, 14 August 1912.
[9] Letter from Kurt Wolff to Franz Kafka, 7 September 1912.
[10] Letter to Felice Bauer, 8 November 1912.
[11] Letter to Felice Bauer, 11 December 1912.
[12] Hans Kohn, "Prager Dichter", *Selbstwehr* (20 December 1912); repr. *Franz Kafka: Kritik und Rezeption zu seinen Lebzeiten 1912–1924*, ed. Jürgen Born (Frankfurt a.M., 1979), p. 18.
[13] Kurt Tucholsky, "Drei neue Bücher", *Prager Tagblatt* (27 January 1913); repr. *Franz Kafka: Kritik und Rezeption zu seinen Lebzeiten 1912–1924*, ed. Jürgen Born (Frankfurt a.M., 1979), p. 20.
[14] Letter to Felice Bauer, 31 January/1 February 1913.
[15] Otto Pick, "Franz Kafka 'Betrachtung'", *Bohemia* (30 January 1913); repr. *Franz Kafka: Kritik und Rezeption zu seinen Lebzeiten 1912–1924*, ed. Jürgen Born (Frankfurt a.M., 1979), p. 22.
[16] Max Brod, "Das Ereignis eines Buches", *März* (14 February 1913); repr. *Franz Kafka: Kritik und Rezeption zu seinen Lebzeiten 1912–1924*, ed. Jürgen Born (Frankfurt a.M., 1979), pp. 24–27.
[17] Letter to Felice Bauer, 14/15 February 1913.
[18] Rudolf Fuchs, "Erinnerungen an Franz Kafka", Max Brod, *Über Franz Kafka* (Frankfurt a.M., 1966), p. 368.

The following books were the source of a number of individual details:

• Binder, Hartmut, *Kafka-Handbuch,* i: *Der Mensch und seine Zeit* (Stuttgart, 1979).
• Hermes, Roger, Waltraud John, Hans-Gerd Koch, and Anita Widera, *Franz Kafka: Eine Chronik* (Berlin, 1999).
• Salfellner, Harald, *Franz Kafka and Prague* (Prague, 2007).

Harald Salfellner
Franz Kafka and Prague

translated from the German
by Anthony Northey,
fully illustrated in colour.
120 pages, 15 x 21 cm,
thread-stitching, softcover.

ISBN 978-80-7253-303-9
9,90 € (Germany)

"Franz Kafka was Prague and Prague was Franz Kafka", Johannes Urzidil once wrote. And indeed, following the traces of Kafka's life, your way leads right into the heart of the old royal seat on the Moldau River.

Every fiber of Kafka's being was rooted in Prague's soil, everywhere in his works the city and its people shine forth between the lines. This compact guide invites its readers into Kafka's world. It teaches you to see Prague as Kafka saw it.

Packed with concise texts and more than 150 historical illustrations, this guidebook has become a Prague classic in its own right: Always up-to-date, for many years and through many editions, it has been the standard reference for all those who are willing to let themselves be guided and carried away: by the poet Franz Kafka and by the Golden Prague of about a hundred years ago.

"Franz Kafka and Prague by Harald Salfellner is by far the best of several works on that subject".
Richard Burton, *Prague. Cities of the Imagination*

ERNST ROWOHLT VERLAG·LEIPZIG

Zur Versendung liegt bereit:

FRANZ KAFKA
BETRACHTUNG

Einmalige Auflage von 800 in der Presse numerierten Exemplaren. — Sorgfältiger Druck auf reinem Hadern-papier durch die Offizin Poeschel & Trepte in Leipzig
In Japan-Broschur M 4.50 — In Halblederband M 6.50

Franz Kafka ist denen, die die Entwicklung unserer besten jungen Dichter verfolgen, längst bekannt durch Novellen und Skizzen, die im »Hyperion« und anderen Zeitschriften erschienen. Seine Eigenart, die ihn dichterische Arbeiten immer und immer wieder durchzufeilen zwingt, hielt ihn bisher von der Herausgabe von Büchern ab. Wir freuen uns das Erscheinen des ersten Werkes dieses feinen, kultivierten Geistes in unserem Verlage anzeigen zu können. Die Art der formal feingeschliffenen, inhaltlich tief empfundenen und durchdachten Be-trachtungen, die dieser Band vereinigt, stellt Kafka vielleicht neben Robert Walser, von dem ihn doch wiederum in der dichterischen Umgestaltung seelischer Erlebnisse tiefe Wesensunterschiede trennen. Ein Autor und ein Buch, dem allseitig größtes Interesse entgegengebracht wird.

Bis 1. Dezember bar bestellt: 40/0/0, Partie 7/6

Wir können der limitierten, einmaligen Auflage wegen à c. nur bei gleichzeitiger Barbestellung und auch dann nur ganz beschränkt liefern.